Playful Animals
PANDAS

Ursula Pang

PowerKiDS press

PK Beginners

Pandas are black and white.

Pandas live near trees.

Some pandas live in zoos.

Pandas eat bamboo.

Pandas climb trees.

Pandas sleep a lot.

Pandas often live alone.

Baby pandas are called cubs.

Pandas are playful!

Pandas are silly!

Pandas are cute!

Published in 2025 by The Rosen Publishing Group, Inc.
2544 Clinton Street, Buffalo, NY 14224

Copyright © 2025 by The Rosen Publishing Group, Inc.

All rights reserved. No part of this book may be reproduced in any form without permission in writing from the publisher, except by a reviewer.

First Edition

Editor: Greg Roza
Book Design: Michael Flynn

Photo Credits: Cover, p. 1 AB Photographie/Shutterstock.com; p. 3 V-yan/Shutterstock.com; p. 5 LP2 Studio/Shutterstock.com; p. 7 awaktepar/Shutterstock.com; p. 9 Daniel X D/Shutterstock.com; pp. 11, 19, 23 Hung Chung Chih/Shutterstock.com; p. 13 SJ Travel Photo and Video/Shutterstock.com; p. 15 Jeroen Mikkers/Shutterstock.com; p. 17 Bbu Kurkovva/Shutterstock.com; p. 21 Foreverhappy/Shutterstock.com.

Library of Congress Cataloging-in-Publication Data

Names: Pang, Ursula, author.
Title: Pandas / Ursula Pang.
Description: [Buffalo] : [PowerKids Press], [2025] | Series: Playful animals
Identifiers: LCCN 2024031256 (print) | LCCN 2024031257 (ebook) | ISBN 9781538312759 (hardcover) | ISBN 9781538312742 (paperback) | ISBN 9781538312766 (ebook)
Subjects: LCSH: Pandas–Juvenile literature.
Classification: LCC QL737.C27 P3488v2025 (print) | LCC QL737.C27 (ebook) | DDC 599.789–dc23/eng/20240705
LC record available at https://lccn.loc.gov/2024031256
LC ebook record available at https://lccn.loc.gov/2024031257

Manufactured in the United States of America

Some of the images in this book illustrate individuals who are models. The depictions do not imply actual situations or events.

CPSIA Compliance Information: Batch #CWPK25. For further information contact Rosen Publishing at 1-800-237-9932.